Focus on History

edited by Ray Mitchell and Geoffrey Middleton

the Time of the Plague and the Fire

Geoffrey Middleton

Headmaster, Colneis County Junior School, Felixstowe

LONGMAN

Every day thousands of people in London pass the places shown on these two pages. But not all know the stories connected with them — stories of two great disasters that happened about three hundred years ago.

Beneath this railed tomb-stone in St Margaret's churchyard, Westminster, lies the body of Alexander Davies, an early victim of a terrible disease which struck London in 1665 and killed over 60,000 people.

In the City, a much larger burial ground is covered by the forecourt of St Mary Abchurch, shown here. In the churchyard which was formerly there, a mass burial of a hundred bodies took place.

This building, in the Strand, bears a plaque which reads:

'The only Strand building to survive the Great Fire of London'.

The Monument stands in the city, not far from London Bridge. It marks a spot close to where a great fire started in 1666. The fire swept through the city and left nearly 200,000 people homeless

To learn more about England at the time of these two disasters we must go back in history over three hundred years; that is, soon after an English king had been executed in public in Whitehall.

The Restoration of the Monarchy

The Restoration of the Monarchy After Charles I was executed in 1649 England had no king for eleven years. For most of this time the country was ruled by Oliver Cromwell, but after his death Prince Charles was invited to return from Holland to become king.

In the picture above Charles is attending a farewell banquet at the Hague, before leaving Holland. He is sitting between the Queen of Bohemia and the Princess Royal.

When Charles Stuart returned to England in May 1660, he was greeted with great enthusiasm by cheering crowds. Church bells pealed, bonfires blazed and guns roared a salute to the new king as he travelled to his palace at Whitehall.

Below you see the royal procession from the Tower of London to Charles' palace on the day before his coronation.

The picture above shows the coronation of Charles II in Westminster Abbey on April 23rd, 1661. After the ceremony a banquet was held at nearby Westminster Hall. This was where his father had been tried for treason and sentenced to death, twelve years earlier.

This medal, which was issued to celebrate the coronation of Charles II, can be seen in the London Museum. Carolus is the Latin name for Charles.

Whitehall Palace lay
between St James's Park
and the Thames, and was
the king's main residence.
This model of it can be
seen in the State
Apartments at Kensington
Palace and although it is
not absolutely accurate it
gives us a good idea of
what the King's Palace
looked like. The key on
the right will help you to
identify the various parts
of the Palace and to
answer the questions on
the page opposite.

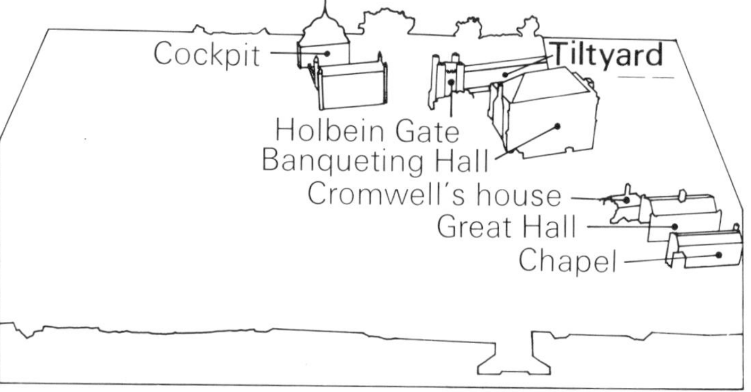

Look again at the model and find:

— the Banqueting Hall which was built by Inigo Jones, a famous architect of Stuart times. This still stands in Whitehall and can be seen in the picture on the left. The remainder of the Palace was destroyed by fire in 1698.

— the Holbein Gate which was the main entrance to the Palace by road.

— the Tiltyard and the Cockpit where the king and his courtiers watched sports, plays and masques.

— Cromwell's House. Oliver Cromwell stopped all entertainment while he lived at the Palace.

Now make your own class model of the Whitehall Palace on a large sheet of hardboard. Some of you can make the various walls and buildings from cardboard, while others can plan the base. Make model boats to put on the river. With clay or plasticine make people for your model.

Samuel Pepys

Samuel Pepys This painting, which is in the National Portrait Gallery, London, is of Samuel Pepys who lived in the City at the time of Charles II.

He held an important position at the Navy Office, but became well known for his diaries. Sometimes he wrote about the people he saw as he walked about the streets. Sometimes he wrote about life in his household.

A page from one of his diaries is shown below, but you will not be able to read it for it is written in a type of shorthand. Perhaps Pepys could write faster this way, or perhaps he did not want everyone to read what he had written. However, many years later, some people were able to decipher it and from it we are able to find out how people lived in those days.

After he had kept a diary for nine years, Pepys thought his eyesight was failing. He was afraid he would go blind if he continued to write each night. So on May 31st, 1669, he wrote the following words:

'And thus ends all that I doubt I shall ever be able to do with my own eyes in the keeping of my journal . . . having done now so long as to undo my eyes almost every time that I take a pen in my hand'.

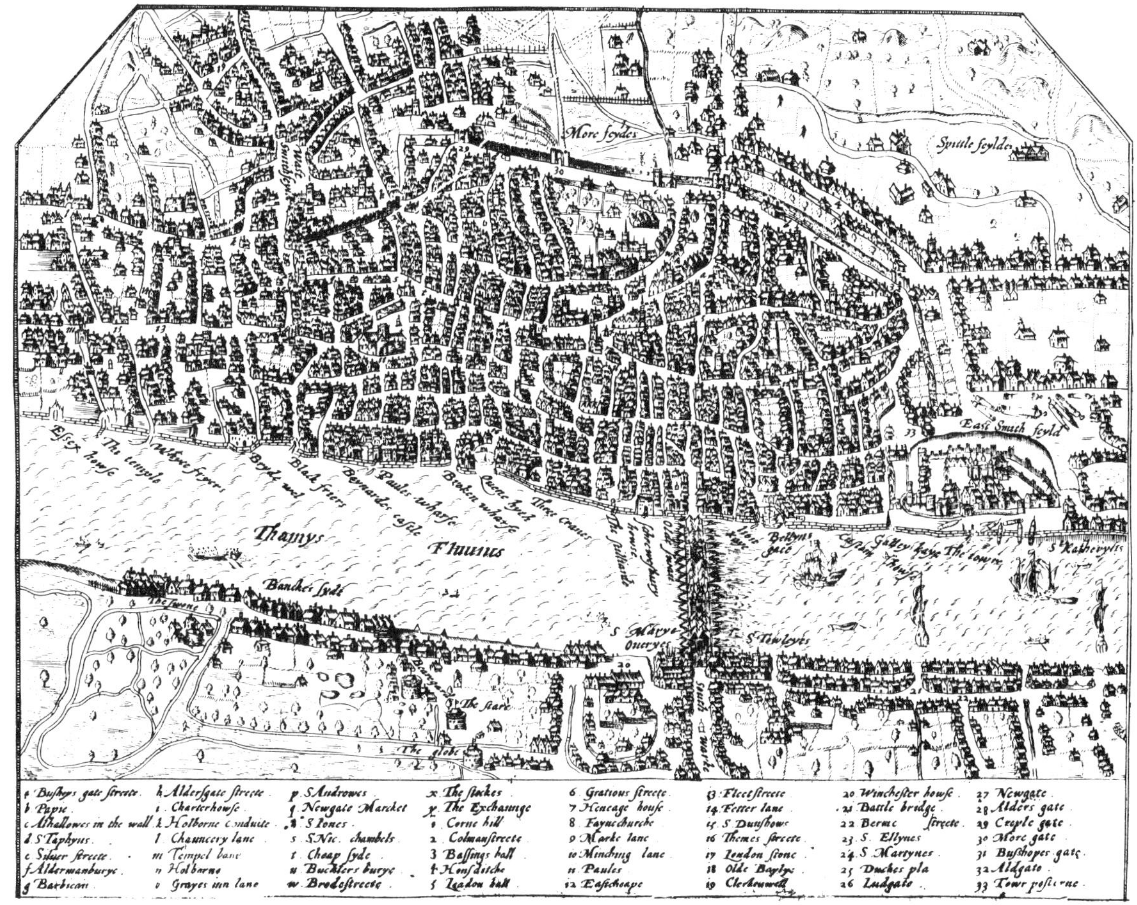

This is a map of London at the time of Samuel Pepys. When Pepys was working at the Navy Office he lived in Seething Lane, not far from the Tower of London. You can see the Tower on the right of the map.

Find the remains of the wall which once stretched round three sides of the city. People entered the city through gates in this wall, but at nightfall the gates were closed. What formed the boundary on the fourth side of the city?

We think there were about 400,000 people living in London at that time, but we are not certain, for records were not always accurate. We do know that more people lived in London than in any other town in England. It was a small city in size, not much more than a mile from one end to the other. But it was densely crowded and had begun to spread outside the walls to the green fields beyond. Chelsea, Knightsbridge and Kensington were then small villages a distance away, and not the large London districts they are to-day.

Town Life
The Streets

This picture of a street in York to-day shows how some town streets looked in Stuart times. In those days, however, they were cobbled with no pavements, but had a gutter down the middle.

People threw their rubbish into the streets where it rotted and stank. In the hot weather it attracted swarms of flies, while at night rats came from their hiding places and burrowed among the decaying rubbish in search of food.

Men called 'rakers' were employed to clear away the rubbish in carts and take it outside the city walls.

Most houses were made of wood and plaster, though the better ones had stone or brick foundations and roofs of red tiles. You can see how the houses leaned over until they almost met those on the opposite side of the street. This made the streets dark and airless.

Many houses were occupied by merchants and shopkeepers. In most large towns there were wool merchants, goldsmiths, saddlers, cutlers, barbers, dyers, pewterers, glaziers, coopers and many others. The front rooms of their houses were used as shops and they had large open windows. These were closed by wooden shutters at night, but during the day the shutters were let down and used as shop counters.

Much trade was carried on by street sellers. 'Fair lemons and oranges,' — 'Four for sixpence, mackerel,' — and 'Pots to mend' were but a few of the loud street cries which echoed down the streets. Above are two other street sellers. What did they sell?

Sedan chairs like this one could be hired in the streets of London. The chair was supported by poles which passed through the rings at the sides. It was carried by two men, one who walked at the front and the other behind the chair.

Towards the end of the 17th century glass replaced the curtained windows at the front and sides of sedan chairs.

It would be easy to make a model of a street in Stuart times. You would need several cardboard boxes of various sizes, some odd pieces of cardboard, and an old blackboard or a sheet of hardboard for a base.

Inside the houses

This was the dining room of a wealthy merchant called Joseph Paine, who became Mayor of Norwich at the time of Charles II. Joseph Paine went to London to present the new king with a thousand pounds in gold as a gift from the City of Norwich. For this he was made a knight.

The oak panelled walls have darkened with age and were very much lighter when Sir Joseph lived there.

The two tall-backed, tapestry covered chairs near the window were called elbow chairs. They were very fashionable at the time of Charles II.

The piece of furniture above was known as a day bed. At one end it had a pad for a head rest. What would we call a day bed nowadays?

But not all people lived in such comfortable conditions as Sir Joseph Paine, the rich merchant. The picture below shows the living room of an ordinary family who lived about the same time. Do you think they lived in the town or the country?

Look carefully at the furniture in this room. The father probably made it himself for his family, as only the rich could afford to have furniture specially made for them by skilled craftsmen.

This family had few possessions. Make a list of those you can see hanging on the wall. Notice the musical instrument hanging near the window and the way the family are dressed. What do you think they will have for their meal? The dog has started his already!

This fireplace was taken from a large farmhouse and can now be seen in the Cambridge Folk Museum.

Look carefully at the picture and find:

the revolving spit used for roasting joints of meat,

the adjustable crane from which pots and kettles were suspended over the fire,

the long-handled frying pan and saucepan.

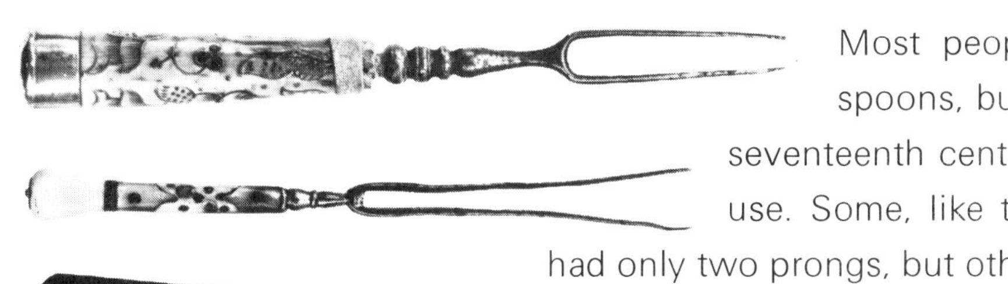

Most people used only knives or spoons, but towards the end of the seventeenth century forks were in general use. Some, like those shown on the left, had only two prongs, but others had three or four. For many years people carried their own forks with them, in a leather case.

Plates and mugs like these were made of pewter, which was a mixture of tin and lead.

This wine bottle, which is in the London Museum, is made of Lambeth Delft ware. It contained sack which was a wine rather like sherry.

The Plague Here is a public fountain, or conduit, which stood at the east end of Cheapside, one of the wider London streets. There were other pumps and conduits elsewhere in the city, and the Aldgate pump (shown in the lower picture) can still be seen to-day.

These conduits were convenient meeting places for the many apprentices and servant girls. They gathered there to fetch water and discuss the latest news or gossip. In the top picture some of them are talking together as they wait to fill their buckets and tankards. Two girls are carrying their bucket suspended from a pole on their shoulders. A water carrier is carrying a tankard on his shoulder. This was quite heavy for it held about five gallons. The carriers were hired to take water to the fine houses of the wealthy.

Water was pumped along pipes to the conduits from the river, into which all kinds of filthy rubbish were often thrown. So it was not surprising that infectious diseases spread rapidly. The most dreaded was the plague, which had already appeared in England many times. During the year 1625, over 40,000 people had died of it in London and people always feared it might return. In the spring of 1665 it did. It was in the parish of St Giles-in-the-Fields, outside the city walls, that it first re-appeared.

On the 7th June, 1665, Samuel Pepys wrote in his diary:

> *'This day, much against my will, I did in Drury Lane*
> *see two or three houses marked with a red cross upon*
> *the doors, and "Lord, have mercy upon us" writ there.'*

The picture above shows a street at the time of the plague. The men carrying the sedan chair are probably taking a sick person to the pest-house. The ladies on the left of the picture are called searchers and are carrying long sticks to warn people to keep away from them. You can read about their work on page 19.

Find the houses with a cross painted on the door, and the watchmen standing on guard outside. Infected houses were shut up until forty days after the sick person had died or been cured. During that time no-one except a doctor or a searcher was allowed to enter or leave the house.

In the picture a dog killer is chasing a dog along the street. By order of the Lord Mayor all dogs and cats were to be killed, for some people thought they carried infection. For each one killed the dog killer was paid twopence. Of course, this was worth much more than it is nowadays.

The Diseases and Casualties this Week.

Abortive	6	Kingsevil	20
Aged	54	Lethargy	1
Apoplexie	1	Murthered at Stepney	1
Bedridden	1	Palsie	2
Cancer	2	Plague	3880
Childbed	23	Plurisie	1
Chrisomes	15	Quinsie	6
Collick	1	Rickets	23
Consumption	174	Rising of the Lights	19
Convulsion	88	Rupture	2
Dropsie	40	Sciatica	1
Drownd two, one at St.Kath. Tower, and one at Lambeth	2	Scowring	13
Feaver	353	Scurvy	1
Fistula	1	Sore legge	1
Flox and Small-pox	10	Spotted Feaver and Purples	190
Flux	2	Starved at Nurse	1
Found dead in the Street at St. Bartholomew the Less	1	Stilborn	8
Frighted	1	Stone	2
Gangrene	1	Stopping of the stomach	16
Gowt	1	Strangury	1
Grief	1	Suddenly	1
Griping in the Guts	74	Surfeit	87
Jaundies	3	Teeth	113
Imposthume	18	Thrush	3
Infants	21	Tissick	6
Killed by a fall down stairs at St. Thomas Apostle	1	Ulcer	2
		Vomiting	7
		Winde	8
		Wormes	18

	Males	83		Males	2656	
Christned	Females	83	Buried	Females	2663	Plague — 3880
	In all	166		In all	5319	

Increased in the Burials this Week —————— 1289

Parishes clear of the Plague —— 34   Parishes Infected —— 96

The Assize of Bread set forth by Order of the Lord Major and Court of Aldermen. A penny Wheaten Loaf to contain Nine Ounces and a half, and three half-penny White Loaves the like weight.

The document on the opposite page is called a Bill of Mortality. These were published every week and this one shows the various causes of deaths in London for the week 15-22 August, 1665. This was when the plague was almost at its worst. It is an interesting document which reveals a great deal of information, but we must remember that it is probably not very accurate.

The information was obtained by the women called searchers. You saw a picture of them on page 17. They had to examine the bodies of all who had died, to find out the cause of their deaths. For this unpleasant task they were paid a fee of one groat, (about fourpence), for each body they examined.

They were often ignorant, unskilled women and although they took an oath to carry out their duties honestly, they sometimes accepted bribes to give false information, for relatives did not wish to reveal there had been plague in the house. Can you think why not?

Look carefully at the Bill of Mortality. How many people died of plague that week? What were the five most common causes of death? The fifth one will probably surprise you.

When you look at the others you will find some strange causes. One person was 'Frighted' and another died 'Suddenly'. Perhaps they had heart attacks. What do you think 'Griping in the Guts' might be called nowadays? You will notice that not many people lived long enough to die as 'Aged'. Even those who did would most likely be under fifty years of age.

The Bill of Mortality on the opposite page records the deaths in each London parish for the same week: 15-22 August, 1665. The first column shows the total number of burials, while the second column gives the number of deaths due to the plague. But these figures may not be accurate. Can you remember why not?

London, although small in size, was a city of many churches. From the Bill find out how many there were within the city walls.

Which parish in the city had most plague deaths that week?

Which parishes had no plague victims at all?

Have you noticed that the 16 parishes outside the city walls had far more plague deaths than the 97 parishes within? Can you think of any reasons for this? Remember that the plague had been raging for three months.

Can you remember in which parish the plague first re-appeared?

What do you notice about the number of plague deaths for that parish on this Bill of Mortality?

The Bill also shows the number of christenings for the week. Why do you think the number is so small? In the picture below you can see a christening ceremony that took place about this time.

Parish	Bur.	Plag.
St Alban Woodstreet	11	8
Alhallows Barking	13	11
Alhallows Breadstreet	1	1
Alhallows Great	6	5
Alhallows Honylane		
Alhallows Lesse	3	2
Alhallows Lumbardstreet	6	4
Alhallows Stayning	7	5
Alhallows the Wall	23	11
St Alphage	18	10
St Andrew Hubbard	1	
St Andrew Undershaft	14	9
St Andrew Wardrobe	21	16
St Ann Aldersgate	18	11
St Ann Blackfryers	22	17
St Antholins Parish		
St Austins Parish		
St Bartholomew Exchange	2	2
St Benner Fynck	2	2
St Benner Gracechurch		
St Benner Paulswharf	16	8
St Benner Sherehog		
St Borolph Billingsgate	2	
Christ Church	27	22
St Christophers	1	
St Clement Eastcheap	2	2
St Dionis Backchurch	2	1
St Dunstan East	7	2
St Edmund Lumbardstr.	2	2
St Ethelborough	13	7
St Faith	6	6
St Foster	13	11
St Gabriel Fenchurch	1	
St George Borolphlane		
St Gregory by St Pauls	9	5
St Hellen	11	11
St James Dukes place	7	5
St James Garlickhithe	3	1
St John Baptist	7	4
St John Evangelist		
St John Zachary	1	1
St Katharine Coleman	5	1
St Katharine Crechurch	7	4
St Lawrence Jewry	2	1
St Lawrence Pountney	6	5
St Leonard Eastcheap	1	1
St Leonard Fosterlane	17	13
St Magnus Parish	2	2
St Margaret Lothbury	2	1
St Margaret Moses	1	
St Margaret Newfishstre.	1	
St Margaret Pattons	1	
St Mary Abchurch	1	
St Mary Aldermanbury	11	5
St Mary Aldermary	2	1
St Mary le Bow	6	6
St Mary Bothaw	1	1
St Mary Colechurch		
St Mary Hill	2	1
St Mary Mounthaw	1	
St Mary Sommerset	6	5
St Mary Stayning	1	
St Mary Woolchurch	1	
St Mary Woolnoth	1	1
St Martin Iremongerlane		
St Martin Ludgate	4	4
St Martin Orgars	8	6
St Martin Outwitch	1	
St Martin Vintrey	17	17
St Matthew Fridaystreet	1	
St Maudlin Milkstreet	2	2
St Maudlin Oldfishstreet	8	4
St Michael Bassishaw	12	11
St Michael Cornhil	3	1
St Michael Crookedlane	7	4
St Michael Queenhithe	7	6
St Michael Quern	1	
St Michael Royal	2	1
St Michael Woodstreet	1	1
St Mildred Breadstreet	2	1
St Mildred Poultrey	4	3
St Nicholas Acons		
St Nicholas Coleabby	1	
St Nicholas Olaves	3	1
St Olave Hartstreet	7	4
St Olave Jewry	1	1
St Olave Silverstreet	23	15
St Pancras Soperlane		
St Peter Cheap	1	1
St Peter Cornhil	7	6
St Peter Paulswharf	5	2
St Peter Poor	3	2
St Steven Colemanstreet	15	11
St Steven Walbrook		
St Swithin	2	2
St Thomas Apostles	8	7
Trinity Parish	5	3

Christned in the 97 Parishes within the Walls — 34   *Buried* — 538   *Plague* — 366

Parish	Bur.	Plag.
St Andrew Holborn	232	220
St Bartholomew Great	58	50
St Bartholomew Lesse	19	15
St Bridget	147	119
Bridewel Precinct	7	5
St Borolph Aldersgate	70	61
St Borolph Aldgate	238	212
St Borolph Bishopsgate	288	236
St Dunstan West	36	29
St George Southwark	80	60
St Giles Cripplegate	847	572
St Olave Southwark	235	131
Saviours Southwark	160	120
S. Sepulchres Parish	403	274
St Thomas Southwark	24	21
Trinity Minories	8	5
At the Pesthouse	9	9

Christned in the 16 Parishes without the Walls — 61   *Buried, and at the Pesthouse* — 2851   *Plague* — 2139

Parish	Bur.	Plag.
St Giles in the fields	204	175
Hackney Parish	12	8
St James Clerkenwel	172	172
St Kath. near the Tower	40	34
Lambeth Parish	13	9
St Leonard Shoreditch	252	168
St Magdalen Bermondsey	57	36
St Mary Newington	74	52
St Mary Islington	50	45
St Mary Whitechappel	319	272
Rotherith Parish	7	2
Stepney Parish	371	273

Christned in the 12 out Parishes in Middlesex and Surrey — 49   *Buried* — 1571   *Plague* — 1244

Parish	Bur.	Plag.
St Clement Danes	94	78
St Paul Covent Garden	18	16
St Martin in the fields	255	193
St Mary Savoy	11	10
St Margaret Westminster	220	191
Whereof at the Pesthouse		13

Christned in the 5 Parishes in the City and Liberties of Westminster — 27   *Buried* — 598   *Plague* — 488

This document is a Royal Proclamation ordering the removal of the King's Exchequer from Westminster to Nonsuch, in Surrey, during the plague. The Royal coat-of-arms is at the top of the document. The King and his Court were no longer at the palace at Whitehall. Where had they moved to? Later, they moved even further away to Oxford, where Parliament also sat.

As the plague spread, many of the nobility, merchants and officials left London with their wives and families. Soon more and more people fled from the horrors of the plague, taking their possessions with them. Only the very poor, the sick, and the dying were left behind. In the picture below, the river Thames is crowded with boats full of people making their escape. The large church in the background is the old St Paul's Cathedral, which was later destroyed by fire.

By the King.

A PROCLAMATION

For removing the Receipt of His Majesties Exchequer from *Westminster* to *Nonsuch*.

CHARLES R.

The Kings most Excellent Majesty taking into his Princely Consideration the great and dangerous increase of the Plague in and about the City of Westminster, where His Majesties Receipt of Exchequer hath been hitherto kept; & willing, as much as is possible, to prevent the further danger to it might ensue as well to His own Officers, which are necessarily to attend the same Receipt, as to other His loving Subjects, who shall have occasion either for Receipt or Payment of Moneys to repair thither, hath therefore taken Order for the present Remove of the Receipt of His said Exchequer, together with the Tally-Office, and all things thereunto belonging from thence to His Majesties Honour of Nonsuch in the County of Surrey: And hath thought fit by this His Proclamation to Publish, That the same shall be there opened on the Fifteenth day of August next, to the end that all persons whom the same may concern, may take notice whither to repair upon all occasions, concerning the bringing in, or issuing out of His Majesties Treasure at the Receipt of His Exchequer. Willing and requiring all Sheriffs, Baylifs, Collectors, and all other Officers Accomptants, and persons whatsoever, who are to pay in any Moneys into the said Receipt of His Majesties Exchequer, or otherwise to attend the same, to keep their days and times at Nonsuch aforesaid, and there to do, pay, and perform in all things, as they should, or ought to have done at Westminster, if the said Receipt of Exchequer had continued there. And this to be done and observed until His Majesty shall publish and declare His further Pleasure to the contrary.

Given at Our Court at *Hampton-Court*, the Six and twentieth day of *July*, 1665. in the Seventeenth year of Our Reign.

God save the King.

LONDON,

Printed by *John Bill* and *Christopher Barker*, Printers to the Kings most Excellent Majesty, 1665.

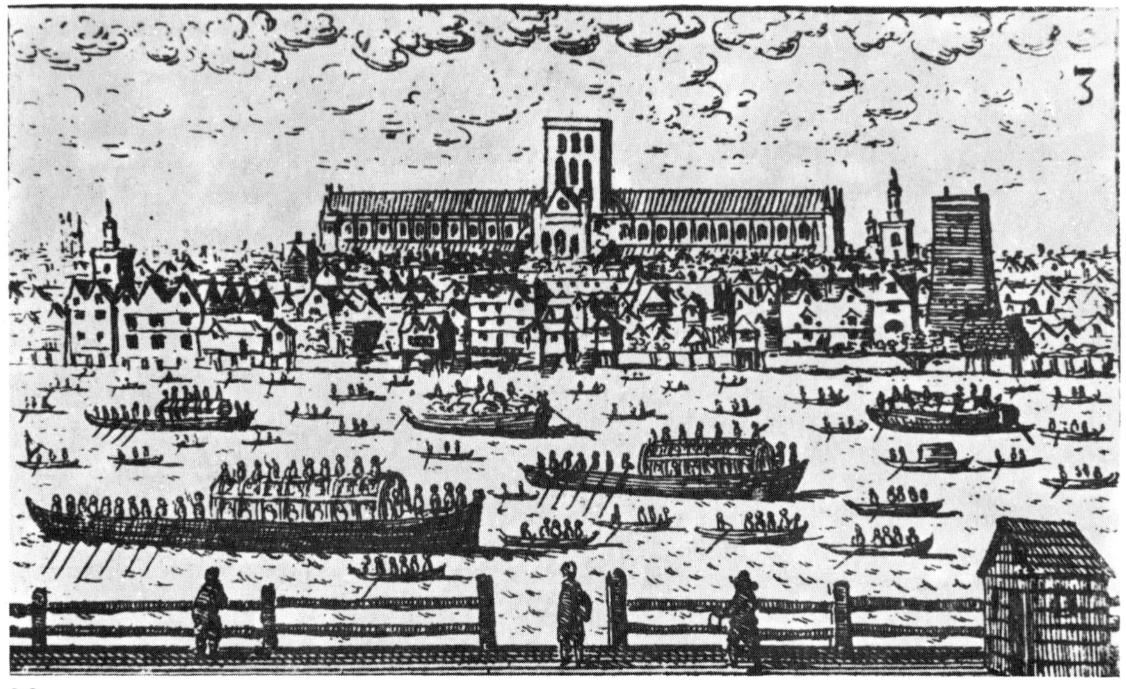

We whose names are hereunto subscribed, doe hereby at the request of this bearer Mary Walker servant to George Bostock of the parish of St. Andrew Undershaft in the Ward of Limestreete in London, Certify such persons whome it may concern, That the said Mary and her Masters whole family and all the Neighbouring Inhabitants of the said Ward are and by Gods blessing have beene all summer free [from] being visited with the infectious disease of the plague or pestilence. In testimony whereof we have sett our hands. Dated the 5th day of July 1665

Richard Hander }
Sam^{ell} Haughton } Churchwardens

These words are taken from a scrap of paper which was a precious possession at the time of the plague. It was a certificate of health to say that a servant girl called Mary Walker was free from the plague. It enabled her to get away from London and find work elsewhere.

Mary must have hid it in the rafters of her attic bedroom for safe keeping, for it was found there when an old inn in Evesham was demolished in 1939. It is now in the Guildhall, in London.

In the picture below, people are leaving London by coach, waggon, on horseback and on foot. Why do you think the guards are stopping them as they approach a nearby town? One man is showing them his certificate of health. What do you think has happened to the man lying near the gate?

The picture on the left shows a costume which was worn by doctors when visiting patients who had the plague. It was made of leather and completely covered the doctor to keep him free from infection.

You can see the mask which covered his head, face and shoulders. The eyepiece was made of glass and the long, beak-like nose was stuffed with perfumes.

The costume must have been very hot and uncomfortable to wear, and it probably scared many of the patients.

Very few doctors stayed in London to fight against the plague and no-one really knew a cure. So people turned desperately to the many quack doctors and pedlars, who recommended all kinds of cures in their efforts to make a quick fortune. Some of their prescriptions were very strange indeed, and many of them hastened the patient's death. Bottles of 'Plague-Water', 'Powdered Unicorn's Horn', and 'Frogs' Legs' were all recommended and sold at outrageous prices. People were prepared to pay a small fortune for a medicine which they thought might cure them.

If you visit the London Museum you will see this old handbell with its wooden handle and iron tongue, or clapper. It was used by the driver of a burial cart to warn people of his approach.

Each parish had its burial cart, which lumbered through the cobbled streets throughout the night, collecting the bodies of those who had died during the day. The clanging of the bell and the driver's hoarse cry of 'Bring out your dead!' struck terror into the hearts of those imprisoned in the plague-infested houses.

At first, the church bells were tolled at the burial of the dead, but soon the ringing was stopped. For as someone wrote: *there die so many that the bell would hardly ever stop ringing and so they ring not at all*.

Soon all the churchyards were full. So huge holes, known as plague pits, were dug on any open space available, often in the fields outside the city walls. Into these the bodies were tipped and covered with earth. In the picture below even the birds are falling dead to the ground.

This statue of a piper and his dog, which is in the Victoria and Albert Museum, London, shows how some people dressed at the time of the plague. Look at the piper's jacket, his knee breeches and long stockings, and his hat.

There is an interesting story about this statue, though we are not certain it is true. It was said that one night a drunken piper fell asleep in a London street. When the burial cart came round in the half light of early morning, the piper was seen lying before the door of a house. It was thought he had been struck down by the plague. So he was tossed into the cart, already piled high with bodies, and carried off to the plague pit, while his dog followed behind.

The jolting of the cart and the barking of his dog awakened the piper, now half sober, just as it became daybreak. He pulled himself upright, dragged out his bagpipes and began to play. The men leading the horses, upon hearing the weird music coming from this strange figure on the loaded cart, fled in fright, saying they had seen the Devil! The piper jumped off the cart and ran back to his lodgings as fast as his legs would carry him. It was said that despite his grim adventure he did not catch the plague.

As the story became known, a sculptor of the period made this statue.

These young children are dancing and singing a well-known nursery rhyme. The first part goes like this:

'Ring a-ring a-roses,
A pocketful of posies'.

This may have been sung at the time of the Great Plague.

The 'ring a-roses' might have referred to the round, red sores on the bodies of those suffering from the plague. The 'pocketful of posies' might have been herbs or spices carried by many people to destroy the dreadful smell of decaying rubbish in the streets. Some ladies carried them in a pomander like the one shown here, others carried scented handkerchiefs.

Here is another part of the rhyme:

' 'Tishoo, 'tishoo,
We all fall down'.

It reminds us that people with the plague often had severe bouts of sneezing. Certainly, most of them collapsed and fell to the ground.

As the cold winter of 1665 approached, the number of deaths fell rapidly. Gradually a few people began to return to the deserted city. The King and his Court returned to Whitehall Palace. The shuttered shops began to re-open and the stricken city came to life again. As Pepys wrote: *'. . . to our great joy the town fills apace and shops begin to be open again'.* But although the epidemic was nearly over, some people continued to catch the plague for a long time afterwards.

The silver spoon below can be seen at the London Museum. It was issued to commemorate the Great Plague of London. If you look closely you will see part of this inscription on the handle: *'Rd in 1665 when dyed at London of the Plague 68,596 — of all Diseases 97,306'.*

These figures were taken from the Bills of Mortality, but it is probable that the actual number of plague deaths was far higher. Thousands more people died in other parts of the country.

Many years later it was found that the plague had been caused by fleas carried by black rats, which scavenged among the filthy rubbish. These rats had swarmed ashore from ships bringing cargoes from the East.

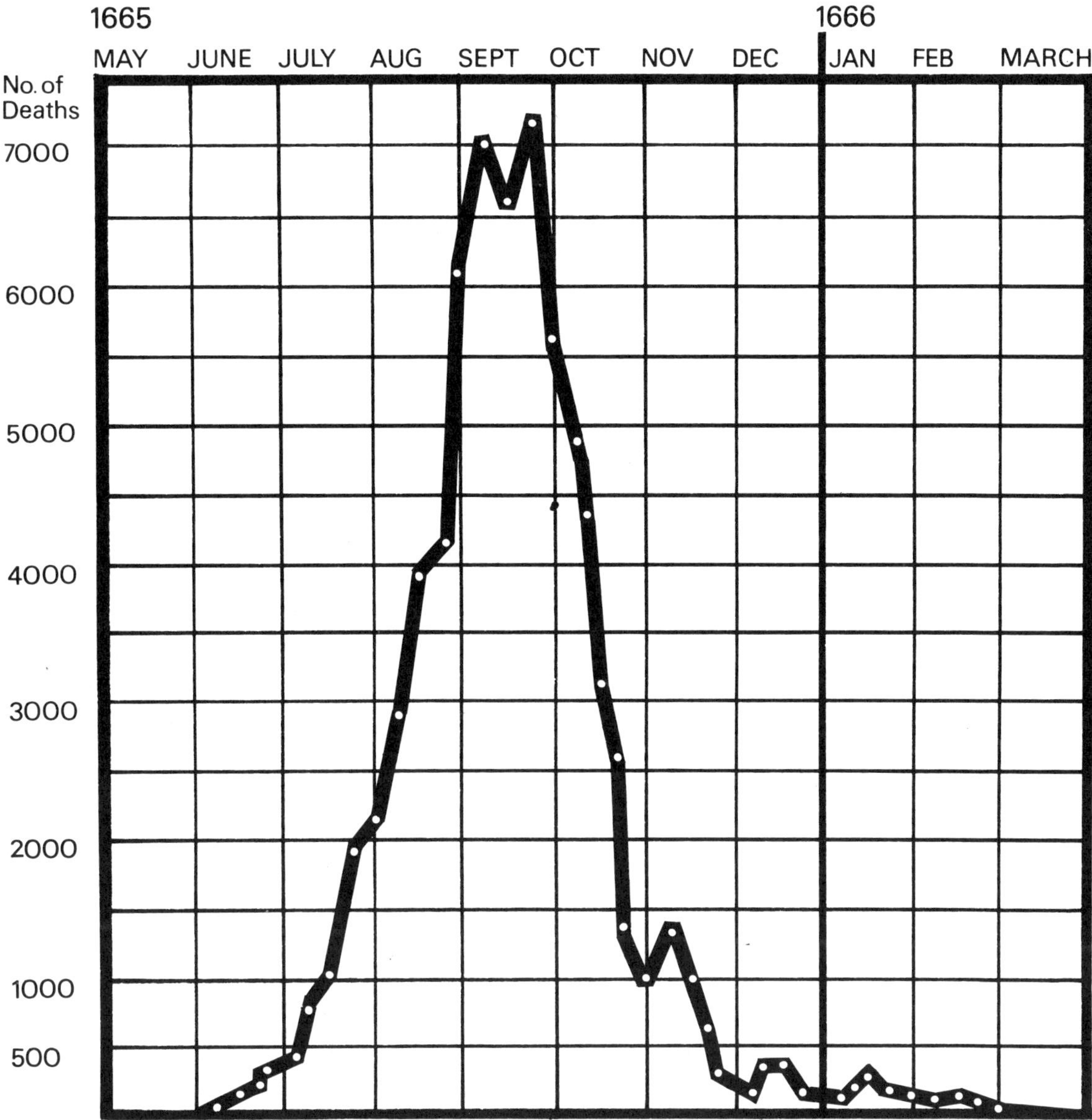

Look carefully at this graph. It shows the number of deaths in London said to be due to the plague. The figures have been taken from the Bills of Mortality for each week. Can you answer the following questions?

When did the epidemic first begin?

In which month did the number of deaths rise most steeply?

In which week were there most deaths? About how many were there?

When did the number of plague deaths fall rapidly?

In which month did the plague stop?

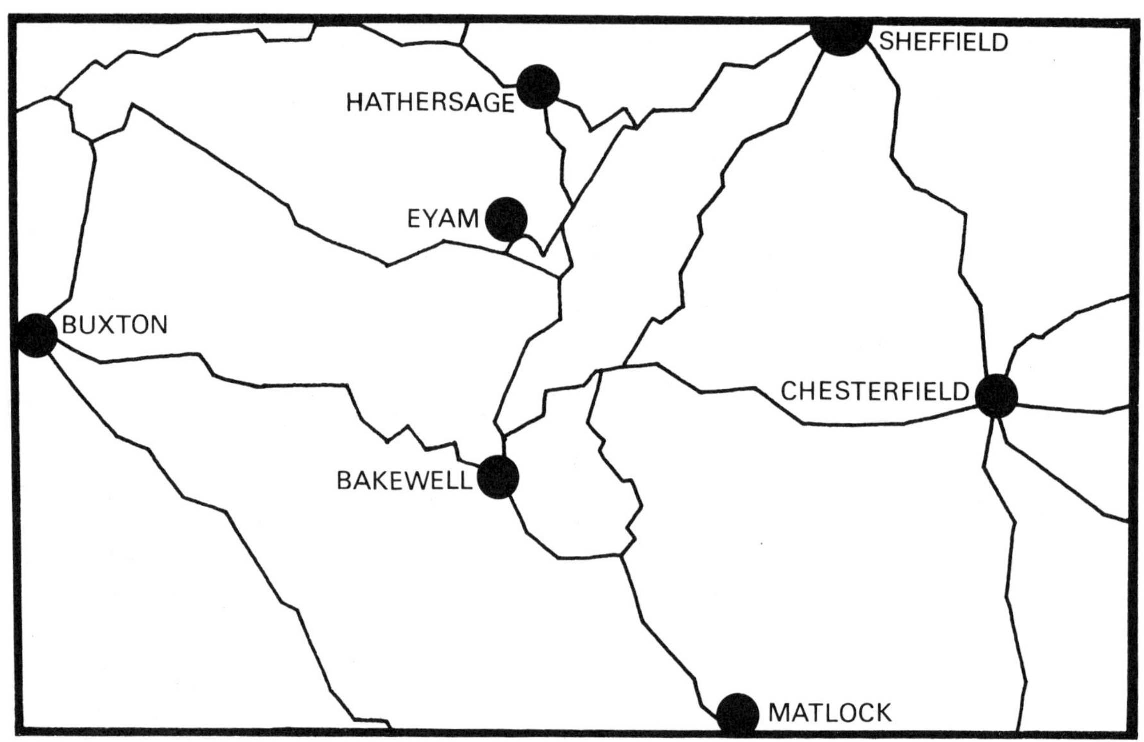

This is a map of a small part of Derbyshire. Can you find a place on it called Eyam? It is a village in the Derbyshire hills with a population of about a thousand people. Three hundred years ago, only about 350 people lived there, together with their rector, William Mompesson.

About the beginning of September 1665, when the plague in London was at its worst, the village tailor received a parcel of clothing from his supplier there. Within a week he was dead. By the end of the month five more villagers had died of the plague, while a further twenty-three deaths occurred during October.

The rector's wife was anxious for the safety of her family and tried to persuade her husband to leave the village. This he refused to do, but he agreed to send their two young children away. The rector and his wife decided to stay behind with their villagers.

The winter months brought frost and snow which helped to check the infectious plague, but by the end of February there had been 22 more deaths and the warmer months were yet to come. The rector realised the dangers which lay ahead. After many arguments he persuaded the villagers to cut themselves off from the rest of the country. No-one was either to enter or leave the village. In this way the infection would be prevented from spreading further. The villagers promised their rector to stay and nearly all of them kept their word.

30

Eyam Church

With the help of the Earl of Devonshire, a large landowner who lived in Derbyshire, William Mompesson arranged for the village to be supplied with food and other provisions. Lists of things needed and the money were placed at the boundary of the village beside a trough filled with water and vinegar. In this the money was washed and disinfected. Supplies were then left for the villagers to collect.

Throughout 1666 the plague continued to spread through the village. The rector decided that meeting in church would only help to spread the infection among his dwindling congregation. So he closed the church and led his people in prayer in the healthier open air of the valley. In August his wife became one of the plague victims, but still the rector stayed on. It was November, 1666, before the plague ended at Eyam, by which time 260 people had died. Less than 100 of the population survived, one of whom was the rector. At that time he wrote:

'Now, blessed be God, all our fears are over for none have died of the plague since the eleventh of October and the pest-houses have long been empty'.

In August each year an open-air service is held in the Delf, as the valley is called, to remember the brave villagers of Eyam.

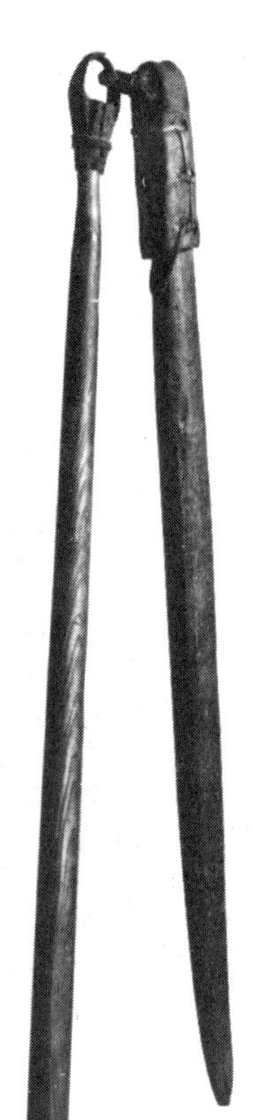

Few farming tools and implements of the 17th century are still in existence to-day. But in some museums we can see tools of a later period which are very similar to those of Stuart times.

So it is probable that tools like those shown on this page were used in villages like Eyam at the time of the plague.

A flail used for beating the ears of corn to separate the grain from the chaff.

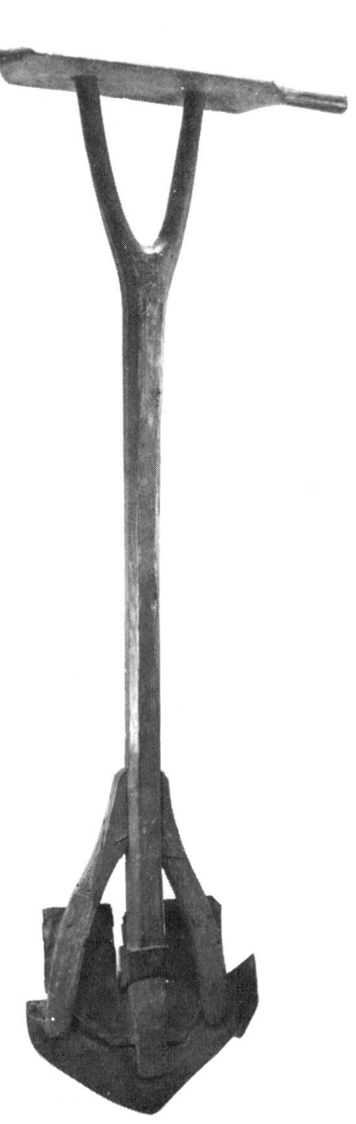

This is a 'breast' plough for removing turf from pasture land. The word 'breast' means turf. The plough was pushed along from the hips, which were protected by a leather apron.

Transport

Transport As trade increased during the seventeenth century, more people found it necessary to travel to other parts of the country. These were often uncomfortable and hazardous journeys for the roads were full of ruts and potholes.

General Directions for the Driver of the Rolling Waggon.

LET the Waggon be greafed as often as you conveniently can, whilft it is new. Be careful that you replace all the Rings or Wafhers, and examine the Boxes often (as they may be liable to get loofe at firft) and wedge them up tight.

Hook up the Back Bands of the Thiller Horfes very fhort,* that the Cattle may draw upwards as much as poffible; and let the Body Horfes (or the Pair next the Thillers) have Pads or Saddles on their Backs, to fuftain the Preffure occafioned by the Leaders.

Load the Waggon forward, and leave the hind Part as light as poffible.

Thefe Precautions obferved, every Owner will find his Account in fuch Carriages, from the very firft; for no Road or Country can prevent their being ufed with Advantage.

Stage waggons like this one travelled on most main roads. They carried goods and also a few passengers who sat among the parcels. Look at the wide wheels. An Act of Parliament ordered them to be at least four inches wide. Can you think why?

The waggoner often walked or rode a separate horse but, despite the frequent use of his whip, the waggon travelled only two or three miles in an hour. A long journey took several days for there were many stops to collect and deliver goods. If the passengers could not afford the price of a room at the inn, they sometimes slept in a hay loft or even in the waggon.

Those who could afford it travelled by stage coach, though these, too, were uncomfortable. Coaches like this had solid iron tyres and no springs. They were suspended on strong leather straps and swayed from side to side as they jolted along the rough roads. At first the windows had no glass, but only a curtain to keep out the draughts. A journey from London to York took four days and cost about £2.

Those travellers who completed their journeys without being stopped by highwaymen were fortunate. For these rogues held up most coaches and robbed their passengers of their money and other valuables. If caught, they were hanged and their bodies were placed by the roadside in a set of irons like those shown on the right. There they were left to rot, as a grim reminder of what would happen to other offenders.

The most famous highwayman of Stuart times was a Frenchman called Claude Duval, who came to England at the time of the Restoration. He was hanged at the age of 27.

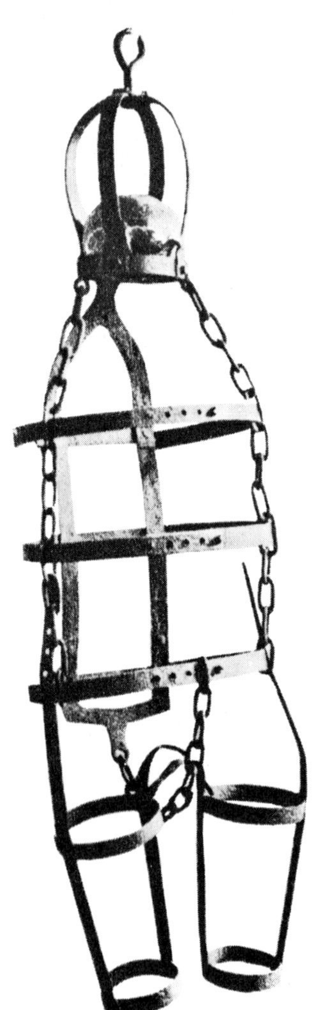

By now you will have a good idea of what it was like to live in England three hundred years ago. So here are some things for you to do:

1 Paint separate pictures of various houses and shops in Stuart times. Cut them out and paste them on large sheets of paper to make a wall frieze of a street. The picture above will help you. Add to your frieze, pictures of a coach and horses, a sedan chair and some people in the street.

2 Make a model in a large cardboard box of Sir Joseph Paine's dining room shown in page 12.

3 Imagine you lived in London at the time of the plague and make an illustrated diary for a week. Write in it some of the things you saw as you walked about the streets and the daily events in your home.

4 Try to find out if there was plague in the district where you live. Your teacher may be able to arrange for you to see your parish records of that time. If not, a visit to your local library or museum may reveal some interesting information.

The Great Fire of London

The model shown on these pages is at the London Museum. It shows another great disaster which struck London only a few months after the plague had died down. This time it was a great fire which, in four days, destroyed over 13,000 houses and 87 parish churches.

During the early hours of Sunday morning, the 2nd September, 1666, a baker and his wife were awakened by the crackling of burning timber. Clouds of smoke were billowing up the staircase of their house in Pudding Lane, not far from London Bridge. The baker's oven in the room below had become overheated and had set fire to the house. The baker, his wife and daughter escaped through a narrow garret window to the house next door — and to safety. The maidservant, terrified at the thought of falling to the cobbled street below, refused to leave the house and was burned to death.

A strong easterly wind blew sparks from the burning building over the houses to the stables of the Star Inn on Fish Street Hill, where they quickly set light to the hay and straw. From there the fire spread to the inn itself.

Soon the timber houses were blazing furiously and the fire was creeping towards the great sheds and warehouses in Thames Street, near the river. These were filled with tallow, spirits, and other inflammable stores.

About three o'clock the Lord Mayor was roused from his bed to see the rapidly spreading fire. He was not pleased at being disturbed, did not think it particularly serious and returned to his bed.

Samuel Pepys was awakened by one of his maids. He writes in his diary:

'Jane called us up about three in the morning, to tell us of a great fire they saw in the city. So I rose and went to the window . . . I thought it far enough off and so went to bed again and to sleep'.

Meanwhile, helped by the strong breeze, the fire continued to spread. Taverns, inns, houses, and even churches went up in flames. There was little time to save personal belongings, or even silver and pewter plate from the churches, though, fortunately, most parish registers and records were saved.

Again, Pepys writes:

'By and by Jane comes and tells me that she hears that above 300 houses have been burned down to-night by the fire we saw, and that it is now burning down all Fish Street, by London Bridge'.

Later, he tells:

'I did see the houses at the end of the bridge all on fire'.

This was at about eight o'clock on the Sunday morning.

Look at this picture of London Bridge as it was during the Great Fire. The houses which Pepys saw burning are those at the end of the bridge. Can you see them? They had been completed only five years earlier, to replace others burned down in a previous fire in 1632.

The long gap in front of the blazing houses prevented the fire from spreading further along the bridge. But the fierce fire also prevented people from escaping across the bridge from the burning city.

In those days there were no fire brigades, but leather buckets like these were provided by each parish. They were kept in the church, usually under the tower, ready for use in the event of fire.

As the great fire spread, men formed a chain of these buckets and emptied them on the flames.

Other men used hand syringes like that shown below. There are several of these in London Museums. It usually took three men to work these syringes — two held the side handles while the third worked the plunger at the end. In this way about a gallon of water could be squirted on the burning buildings, but the jet of water would not reach any great height.

As Pepys walked about the streets he could see that these attempts to put out the flames were having little effect and the fire was spreading rapidly. People were more concerned with trying to save their own possessions than dealing with the fire. So Pepys went to see the King at Whitehall Palace.

Pepys writes:

'The King commanded me to go to my Lord Mayor and command him to spare no houses, but to pull down before the fire every way'.

Iron fire hooks like this were fastened to long poles and were used for pulling down houses which stood in the path of the fire, to stop it from spreading. But normally, this could not be done before the flames reached the houses, or else the person responsible would have to pay for the cost of rebuilding.

The hook was thrown over the ridge-beam of the building, ropes were fastened to iron rings at the end of the pole, and teams of men or horses heaved and pulled until the house came crashing to the ground. Then the piles of thatch, plaster and timber had to be cleared away before the rapidly approaching fire reached them. Often it was too late and the demolished houses merely added fuel to the flames.

The leather helmet below was used by a fireman when fighting the Great Fire. It belonged to the parish of St George's, Billingsgate. St George's was one of the many churches destroyed by the fire.

By Monday morning the fire had reached the heart of the city and people began to panic. The streets were jammed with handcarts and barrows, piled high with pieces of furniture and personal belongings, as people tried to escape.

Thomas Vincent, a writer of that time, wrote:

'– any money is given for help, five, ten, twenty, thirty pounds for a cart . . .'.

This painting is how an 18th century artist called P. J. de Loutherbourg imagined the crowded Thames must have looked. The watermen had been busy throughout the night ferrying people and their goods across to the southern bank of the Thames, or further up the river beyond the reach of the flames.

Paint your picture of how you imagine the crowded streets must have looked at this time. Remember to include the handcarts, the attempts to fight the fire and the houses being demolished.

In this picture the fire has reached the old St Paul's Cathedral. Because there were open spaces around St Paul's, nearby stationers and booksellers had carried their goods into the church. They thought they would be safe there, particularly in the crypt and vaults below. But the strong wind carried burning embers to the roof and soon the huge cathedral was ablaze.

In the letter below, which can be seen at the London Museum, the writer describes King Charles II and the Duke of York.

'handing the water in buckets when they stood up to the ankles in water and playing the engines for many hours

Another writer says:

'they gave orders for blowing up of houses with gunpowder, to make spaces for the fire to die in'.

Late on Tuesday night the wind dropped and the fire was checked. By Thursday, 6th September, it was practically out and London was a wilderness of smouldering, charred ruins. John Evelyn, walking through the city, said:

'I clambered over mountains of smoking rubbish and . . . the ground under my feet so hot it even burnt the soles of my shoes and put me all over in sweat'.

Thousands of people were homeless and camped in the fields outside the city. Next day the King rode out to speak to them and promised them help. Arrangements were made to protect their possessions and to send them food supplies. Some people soon returned to live in their cellars.

Although several plans for building a new city were submitted to the King and his Council they were considered too difficult to adopt. But building in the ruins was forbidden until all rubbish and ashes had been cleared from the roadway in front. All new buildings were to be of brick and stone. Can you think why? Any new building scheme needed a special permit like that shown above. This was issued by Charles II and you can see a fragment of the King's Great Seal at the foot of the document.

The badges on this page are fire-marks of various fire insurance companies. At the time of the Great Fire there was no such thing as fire insurance. People whose homes were destroyed had to find the money themselves to build a new one.

Gradually, fire insurance companies were formed and people began to pay regularly small sums of money to them. In the event of fire they could then claim payment for any damage they had suffered.

Naturally the insurance companies wanted to avoid paying out money if possible. So they formed their own fire-brigades which would only attend fires at properties insured with their companies. A fire-mark was fixed to the front of a building to show the fire-brigade that it was insured. It was usually placed at a good height from the ground to avoid being stolen. Each company had its own fire-mark and sometimes it had the number of the insurance policy stamped on it. Can you find any fire-marks on the old buildings in your town?

44

Christopher Wren

This carving of Sir Christopher Wren is in the National Portrait Gallery. He was an architect who became Surveyor General soon after the Great Fire. Wren submitted a plan for a new London but, like the others, it was rejected.

During the fire 84 of the 109 churches in the city were destroyed and three others were severely damaged. It was decided to reduce the number of parishes, but even so 51 new churches were to be built, and Wren was given the task of designing them.

St Bride's in Fleet Street is one of them and is sometimes known as the 'wedding-cake' church. Can you think why? Can you remember the churchyard mentioned on page 2 where the plague victims were buried? The church shown there was also built by Wren, for the original church was destroyed in the fire.

This house on the south bank of the Thames is called Wren's house. From here, the story goes, he watched the new St Paul's rise from the ashes of the old cathedral on the other side of the river.

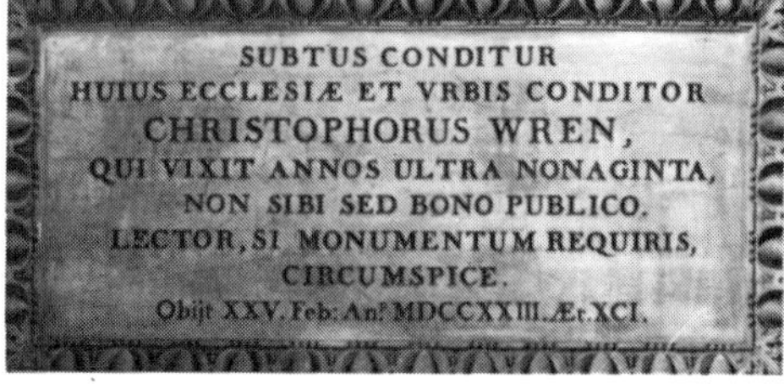

Sir Christopher Wren's greatest memorial is his St Paul's Cathedral which took 35 years to build. After his death he was buried in the cathedral. This Latin inscription is above his tombstone, and tells us to look around if we would see his monument.

If we climb the many steps to the Stone Gallery outside the dome the city of London lies below us. We can see, not only the spires and towers of Wren's churches, but also the Monument erected within a few yards of the baker's shop were the Great Fire first started.

46

Now that you have finished reading this book here are some more things for you to do.

1 Make a model of London in Stuart times.

First draw a plan of the main streets on a large piece of strawboard or hardboard. Then add the city walls, the gates which led into the city, London Bridge and the river Thames.

You will find it easier to make solid houses, (rather like those used in the game of 'Monopoly'). Larger buildings, such as the Tower of London and St Paul's, can be made from matchboxes, and the city walls from cardboard or strips of wood. You can use balsa wood for London Bridge. Don't forget to put some boats on the river.

2 Paint the following pictures of the Great Fire of London to make a wall frieze for your classroom:

> The baker and his wife escape from their burning house;
> Early attempts to put out the fire with buckets and squirts;
> Houses being pulled down with fire hooks;
> Streets crowded with people trying to save their possessions;
> Escape by river;
> The fire from the South bank of the river;
> Houses being blown up with gunpowder by the soldiers;
> King Charles speaking to the refugees.

Write some sentences about each picture and paste them underneath.

3 Write a letter to a friend in the country about your adventures during the Great Fire.

4 Plan an exhibition in your classroom of your models, friezes and other work. Invite children from other classes to see it and tell them about it.

Index